BRAIN GAMES®

Goes to the D🐾GS
PICTURE PUZZLES

Publications International, Ltd.

Image Sources: Dreamstime, Mollie Firestone, Fotolia, Rebecca Gizicki, iStockphoto, Jupiterimages Unlimited, Photodisc, Shutterstock.com, Superstock

Contributing Writers: Holli Fort, Laura Pearson

Front cover puzzles: *Hot Chihuahua!,* see page 133; *A Plethora of Pillows,* see page 45. Back cover puzzle: *Pooch on Parade,* see page 19.

Louis Weber, CEO
Publications International, Ltd.
8140 Lehigh Avenue
Morton Grove, IL 60053

Permission is never granted for commercial purposes.

ISBN-13: 978-1-4508-0367-0
ISBN-10: 1-4508-0367-9

Manufactured in China.

8 7 6 5 4 3 2 1

Beware: Doggone Tricky Changes Ahead! ■ 4

These easy puzzles will open your eyes to the joys of picture puzzles!

Look a little more closely at these delightful images.

Be on guard for more subtle changes in this section.

Look closely to sniff out the changes in these challenging puzzles.

Beware: Doggone Tricky Changes Ahead!

Are you ready to be put to the test? The picture puzzles in this book run the gamut from sweet to fun to quirky—and they also challenge your mind. Just look carefully at the pictures on each page to see if you can spot the differences between them. But don't let your guard down! The puzzles get progressively harder with each level. The number of changes increases, the differences become more subtle, and the pictures are more densely detailed.

As you move through the book, you'll hone your observational skills. Keep in mind that we've altered each picture in a variety of ways. You might find a dog has changed his spots, a ball has disappeared, a shadow or reflection has been altered, or a tree has appeared. Some puzzles demand that you pay extra attention, as the changes may be found in the smallest details.

Not all puzzles feature just two images. Some involve finding a single change among a grouping of four or six of the same picture. You'll need to look carefully to discover which picture is not like the others.

Check your work with the answer key at the back of the book. The original picture is presented in black and white, with the changes circled and numbered.

Putting your brain to work and focusing your attention are great ways to find fun, enjoyment, and challenge during your day. So take a deep breath, clear your mind, and get ready to find all the differences in *Brain Games*®: *Goes to the Dogs Picture Puzzles*!

Pondside Pals

Scan these sweet shepherds and see if you can find all the differences.

Puppy Surprise!

Some differences popped up in one of these pictures.
Can you pick them all out?

Answers on page 169.

Life's a Beach

...at least for these big dogs! Sit back, relax,
and see if you can uncover some changes.

Steer Clear!

Every dog has its day, and clearly this dog is having his! How many differences do you detect?

Answers on page 169.

Dedicated Guard Dog

Enliven this bulldog's day by finding the single change
among the pictures below.

1

2

3

4

5

6

Swingin' Around

By now you're getting into the swing of solving these
puzzles. Can we push you to solve this one?

Answers on page 169.

Connect the Dots

One of these pictures is dotted with differences. Look closely!

Picture This!

Look closely and you'll discover some differences—
just like these dogs have discovered the camera!

Oh, Deer!

Take a look at these holiday hounds and see if you can unwrap some differences.

Answers on page 170.

Take Five

Give this puzzle *paws,* and see if you can find a few differences.

A Shaggy-Dog Story

Examine this pink-wearing pair and see if you can spot some differences.

Answers on page 170.

Hit the Road

This fun-loving dog was clearly born to ride.
Scan the scene for all the changes we've made.

Best in Show

Locate a single change in one of these pictures
and you'll get the red-carpet treatment!

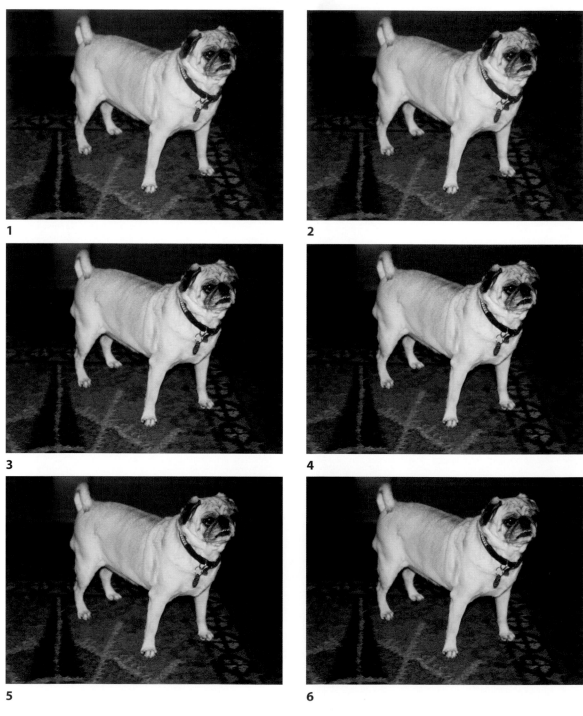

1

2

3

4

5

6

Answer on page 171.

Pooch on Parade

We've dressed up one of these photos. Don't let any changes pass you by!

Time to Play

See if you can find the playful changes we've made to this outdoor scene.

Well-Dressed Doggie

This Pekingese is dressed to the nines! Can you find
all the flourishes we've added to this photo?

Answers on page 171.

Grin and Bear It!

One of these pictures is stuffed with changes. Wrestle with this
puzzle for a bit, and we're sure you'll find them all!

Hot Diggety Dog!

Don't let this cute puppy drive you to distraction. Focus on finding a single change in one of the pictures below.

1

2

3

4

5

6

Answer on page 171.

Down at the Dog Beach

Survey this sandy beach and this sandy-colored dog,
and see if you can dig up some differences.

Shift into Gear

You might not automatically solve this puzzle, but we know
you'll find all the changes if you just stay focused!

Answers on page 172.

Let Sleeping Dogs Lie

Settle into your favorite spot and see if you can solve this puzzle.
We're sure you're intent on finding all the differences!

Midnight Snack

Hungry for a challenge? Take a bite out of this puzzle by
finding all the differences between these pictures.

Bench Buddies

We've tossed some changes into this picture. Can you retrieve them all?

Answers on page 172.

Chew on This

No need to shake in your boots! Finding a single change
in one of these pictures should be a cinch.

1

2

3

4

Not a Care in the World

Hop in, find the differences, and then cruise on to the next puzzle!

Answers on page 173.

Twin Terriers

These pictures may look similar, but just like these terriers,
they differ slightly. Can you find all the changes?

Take a Seat

... and see if you can solve this puzzle. Don't sweep this challenge under the rug!

Sea Change

We've altered one of these oceanside scenes. Can you find all the differences?

Answers on page 173.

Behind the Wheel

Compare these canine chauffeurs and see if you can spot a single difference.

1

2

3

4

5

6

Answer on page 173.

Lawn Chair Lounging

Here's a relaxing puzzle for you. See if you can find
four differences between these images.

Answers on page 173.

On the Dottie

Can you spot the differences we've made to this adorable dalmatian?

Bird's-Eye View

Apparently, this parrot and pooch see eye-to-eye. Some differences should come into focus as you stare at these pictures.

Answers on page 174.

Don't Fence Me In!

There are some differences between these pictures, and we
feel certain you'll jump at the chance to find them!

Animal Print

Get yours paws on this puzzle, and see if you
can find all the changes we've made.

Orchard Stroll

Some changes have blossomed in one of these pictures. Sniff them out!

Answers on page 174.

A Plethora of Pillows

This pillowy scene was nearly perfect, but we did make
some minor adjustments. Can you find them all?

Dem Bones

Something about these pictures just doesn't add up.
Can you find all the differences?

Answers on page 175.

Pooch Patrol

Solving this puzzle won't be a walk in the park!

It Takes Two to Play a Tango

Hit all the right notes by finding all the changes.

Morning, Joe!

Finding the single change among these photos is sure to perk you right up!

1

2

3

4

5

6

Answer on page 175.

Chill Chaser

Snow little accomplishment to find all the differences below!

Homework Helper

Study this picture carefully to find all the changes.

Answers on page 175.

Master Hurdler

You may run into a few obstacles trying to navigate this puzzle.

Go with the Flow

It may take some dogged determination, but we're sure
you'll find all the differences between these photos.

Answers on page 176.

Hot Dogs

You're sure to be fired up after you find all the changes below!

Santorini Snoozer

Be on your guard—some changes have crept up in the scene below.

Dog House Delight

Search carefully, and before you know it, you'll be
in the home stretch of this puzzle!

Answers on page 176.

Bird-dogging Blast

Can you catch the single change hidden among these photos?

1

2

3

4

5

6

Answer on page 176.

Bichon Frise Frame

You might want to read up on the latest methods before attempting this puzzle.

Answers on page 177.

Glamour Shots

Strike a pose, and then get down to the business of solving this puzzle.

Canine Express

Get on board to find all the differences between these photos.

Answers on page 177.

Crowd Control

You'll need to keep your concentration on a tight leash for this puzzle.

Gate Guard

Don't lie down on the job! Find the single difference among these photos.

1

2

3

4

5

6

Answer on page 177.

Telling *Tails* Out of School

There's no way to whitewash it—we've made a lot of changes to this scene.

How Fetching!
Stop by and catch all the latest changes.

A Tired and True Friend

Some are obvious, but can you spot the rest of the changes?

Answers on page 178.

Beachside Barker

You shouldn't have too *ruff* of a time finding the changes in the scenes below.

Playful Par-Tea

You are cordially invited to find the single change
we've hidden among these photos.

1

2

3

4

5

6

Answer on page 178.

Watch Dog

Look closely to find the differences between the shots below.

Dog Tired
Make sure you exhaust all options before giving up on this puzzle.

Answers on page 178.

Chaise-ing After Changes

No time for lounging! It's time to solve this puzzle.

Puppy Love

This little fella doesn't look like he could cause too much trouble;
we're sure you can wrap this one up neatly!

Grooming Spot

Spotting changes: A habit that won't take you to the cleaners.

Answers on page 179.

Autumnal Array

Think you can find the single change hidden in one
of these photos? We'll *leaf* you to it.

1

2

3

4

5

6

Answer on page 179.

Costume Caper
This party has gone to the dogs!

Answers on page 179.

Short Sale

Solving this one will be a real treat!

Saturday in the Park

Can you run down a full list of changes?

Answers on page 180.

A Day at the Beach

Comb this sandy scene for changes.

Answers on page 180.

Protective Pup

You may need a magnifying glass
for this Neighborhood Watch project.

Belles of the Balls

Put a *paw*sitive spin on things by serving up all the changes.

Answers on page 180.

Throw a Dog a Bone

You're sure to have a bone to pick with this puzzle.

End of the Road

Changes have flooded into this section of town. How many can you find?

Answers on page 180.

Just Lounging

Case this scene thoroughly to catch all the differences.

Flowery Flight

Changes are budding all over this picture!

Lucky Lookout

Keep a sharp eye out for the single change
lurking among these photos.

1

2

3

4

5

6

Answer on page 181.

Now Look Here!

This dog is all too aware of the changes that have been made to this serene scene.

High Net Worth

You're sure to get all caught up in this puzzle.

Answers on page 181.

Housing Development

Can you build up a full list of the differences here?

Step It Up

You'll need to *stair* closely to find some of the changes below.

Training Exercise

Attack this puzzle, and find all the changes.

Answers on page 182.

Sticking Together

We've stuck one change in among these photos. Can you spot it?

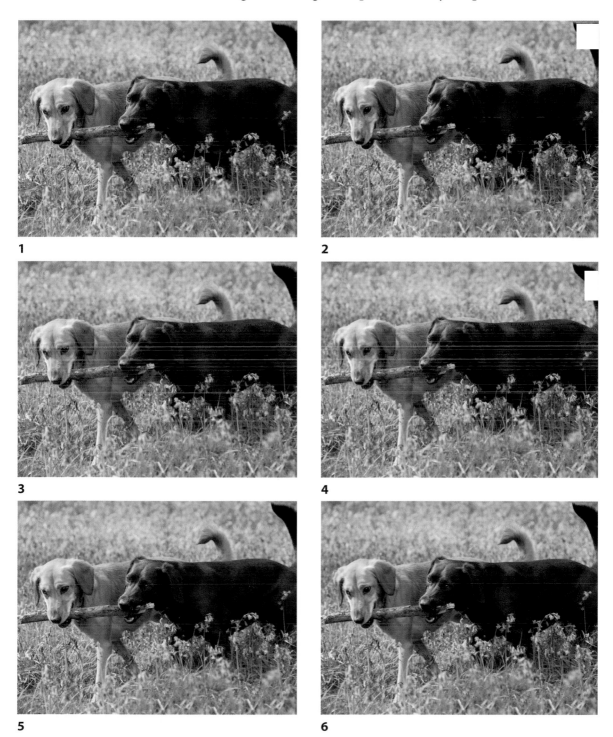

1

2

3

4

5

6

TV for Two

Watch carefully as we present a full schedule of changes.

Answers on page 182.

Playground Pals

Don't get shut out of all the fun—play around until you've found all the changes.

Answers on page 182.

Barnyard Blitz

Stand up and count the changes.

Answers on page 182.

The World at His Paws

We're *pawsitive* you can spot all the changes below.

Hydrant and Seek

Find a nice, out-of-the-way spot,
then get ready to find all the changes!

Puzzling Paw-ty

Join in on the fun, and find all the changes hidden below.

Pup Tent Puzzler

Can you sniff out the single change
camouflaged among these photos?

1 change

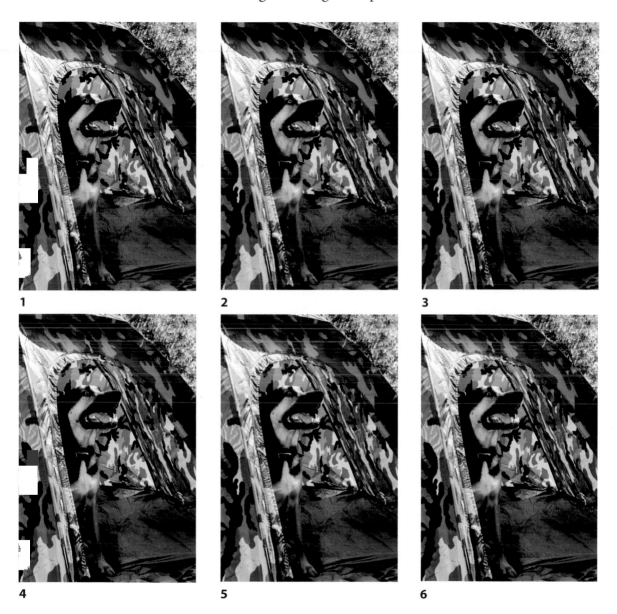

1

2

3

4

5

6

Night at the Circus

It started as a flea circus, but the dogs stole the show!
Can you show them up by pointing out all the changes?

Answers on page 183.

Welcoming Committee

You'll need to step up your efforts to find all the changes below.

Recreational Vista

Don't overlook the changes below.

Answers on page 184.

Farmer's Helper

We're not trying to entice you to buy anything—just scan these photos and make a list of all the changes you find.

Soggy Scene

Studying these photos will surely *wet* your appetite for puzzles!

Just Horsing Around

No time for grazing! Get to work and find the single change among these photos.

1

2

3

4

5

6

Answer on page 184.

Promenade Rambler

You may need to shop this one around to detect every change.

Pier-bred Pooch

We're *moor* than sure you can find all the differences between these photos.

Answers on page 184.

Drive-Thru Service

Pull in and search for changes. Be sure to look at these photos from every angle.

Required Reading

Take a load off—but be on the alert for changes.

Answers on page 185.

Cruise Control

This puzzle's a real classic!

Let Them Eat Cake

Finding all the changes below
would be the icing on the cake!

Street Serenade

Accordion to our count, there are quite a few changes to be found here.

Answers on page 185.

Riff Raft

You'll need to go with the flow to solve this puzzle.

One Dog Night

Cozy up with your favorite furry friend and take a close look at this scene.

Answers on page 186.

Dapper Dogpatch

Can you hunt down the single change hidden among these photos?

1

2

3

4

5

6

Stair Down

Keep your eyes on the prize and find all the changes below.

Answers on page 186.

Street Stroll

Unleash your energy and line up all the differences.

Sheepdog Search

Don't feel sheepish if you can't find all the changes
right away—you may be in for a long ride.

Answers on page 186.

Leashed Looker

It's okay to stare—we know you're just trying to find all the changes!

Answers on page 186.

Dogs Agog!

We don't mean to bark orders, but please scan this
sunny field and find all the differences.

Hot Dog!

Pinpoint all the changes in these colorful scenes, and you'll surely be top dog.

Answers on page 187.

Lying Low

The time to act is now! Find the single change among the pictures below.

1

2

3

4

5

6

Answer on page 187.

131

Perplexing Path

One of these paths is not like the other. Follow your
instincts to arrive at the differences.

Answers on page 187.

Hot Chihuahua!

Make a splash by finding all the differences we've
made to this shot of a poolside pooch.

Shop 'Til You Drop
Find all the modifications we've made, and this puzzle will be in the bag!

Porch Pooch

If you don't feel like running with the big dogs,
stay on the porch and be on your guard for changes.

Answers on page 188.

Leader of the Pack

One of these pictures is packed with changes.
Master this puzzle by finding them all.

Polka Dot Pup

Can you spot a single difference in one of these pictures?

1

2

3

4

5

6

Answer on page 188.

It's a Dog's Life

Survey these scenes, and see if you can sniff out some differences.

Rake in the Differences

We hope you're not dog-tired and can help with a little yard work:
Your chore is to find all the differences between these pictures.

Answers on page 188.

Home Improvements

We've redecorated this room. Can you find all the modifications we've made?

Dog on Board

Can you find all the changes we've made to this canine
in a canal boat? Don't let any float by!

LEVEL 4

10 changes

Dog Days of Summer

This puzzle is no picnic, but if you look carefully,
we think you can spot all the differences.

Answers on page 189.

Summertime Stroll

Paws a moment, and see if you can detect the single change among these photos.

1

2

3

4

5

6

Labrador of the Lake

We've altered this serene scene in numerous ways.

Answers on page 189.

Mush!

Harness your puzzle-solving skills to see if you can find
all the differences between the scenes below.

Nobody Gets Past Me!

Survey this display (and serious security guard!),
and see if you can find all the modifications we've made.

Did Somebody Say "Biscuit"?

Take a close look at these distracted pups,
and see if you can spot some differences.

Answers on page 190.

Puzzling Plaza

Doggone it—one of these plazas is not like the other!
Can you chase down all the changes?

Hair of the Dog

Groom your puzzle-solving skills by detecting all
the differences in the scenes below.

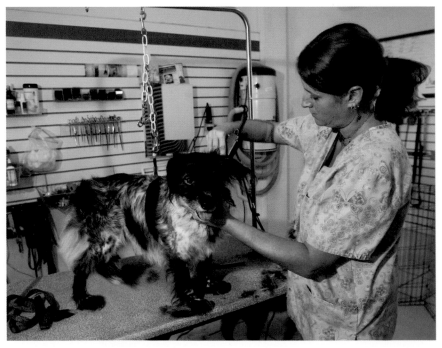

Answers on page 190.

Horsin' Around

We don't mean to hound you, but can you find all the
differences we've made to this pastoral scene?

Woman's Best Friend?

This pooch certainly completes this ensemble! See if you can
pick up on all the changes we've made to this scene.

Answers on page 190.

Teatime for Terriers

You're the lucky dog who gets to find all the modifications we've made to this prim and proper setting! One lump or two?

Answers on page 190.

Rise to the Occasion

Build on your puzzle-solving experience, and see if you can hunt
down all the changes among these high-rise buildings.

Riverside Walk

Some changes lurk ahead. How many will you stumble upon?

Answers on page 191.

Down on the Farm

You don't need to work like a dog to find all the changes
we've made, but you do have to look closely!

Out for a Stroll

Walk right up and detail all the differences between these photos.

Answers on page 191.

Rein in the Changes

Finding all the differences here shouldn't be as challenging
as the Iditarod, but make sure you stay focused!

Down by the Bay

These cute collies are enjoying a day at the marina. Can you locate some differences? (We're *shore* you can!)

Answers on page 191.

Rest Stop

These pups are patiently waiting for you to find
the single change among these photos.

1

2

3

4

5

6

Not Your Typical Fire Dog

Not to add fuel to the fire, but there are some differences stationed throughout these pictures. Can you find them, now that the smoke has cleared?

Take a Walk

We've unleashed some changes in one of these pictures. Can you spot them all?

Answers on page 192.

Westward, Ho!

Can you corral all the differences we've made to this canine cowboy?

Don't Be Sheepish

We think you can solve this puzzle in two shakes of a lamb's tail! Just look carefully.

Answers on page 192.

LEVEL 1

Pondside Pals, *(page 5)* **1.** Tree reflection disappeared; **2.** bone on collar enlarged; **3.** pole became thicker; **4.** tree moved right; **5.** reflection of tree moved down.

Puppy Surprise!, *(page 6)* **1.** Flower deleted; **2.** collar turned yellow; **3.** nose grew bigger; **4.** flowers erased; **5.** rope disappeared.

Life's a Beach, *(page 7)* **1.** Orange part of umbrella disappeared; **2.** post erased; **3.** shoe appeared; **4.** umbrella pole thicker; **5.** more of leg became brown.

Steer Clear!, *(page 8)* **1.** Hill became higher; **2.** red bar added; **3.** white part of seat turned red; **4.** brown spot expanded.

Dedicated Guard Dog, *(page 9)* **1.** Bowl shrunk in picture 4—did his owner put him on a diet?

Swingin' Around, *(page 10)* **1.** Shadow grew; **2.** tongue longer; **3.** hook flipped; **4.** trees grew taller.

Connect the Dots, *(page 11)* **1.** Twig added; **2.** red splotch erased; **3.** white area on ear turned black; **4.** spot deleted.

Take Five, *(page 15)* **1.** White fur turned black; **2.** silver ring disappeared from leash; **3.** another zipper appeared; **4.** red sock grew taller; **5.** another snap appeared.

Picture This!, *(pages 12–13)* **1.** Part of fence disappeared; **2.** dog's ear shorter; **3.** building taller; **4.** cloud grew bigger; **5.** pink section of wall expanded.

A Shaggy-Dog Story, *(page 16)* **1.** Rocks added to ledge; **2.** another buckle appeared; **3.** pink cuff grew longer; **4.** boot taller; **5.** rose erased.

Oh, Deer!, *(page 14)* **1.** Nose turned black; **2.** ribbon end erased; **3.** another red ornament appeared; **4.** white bow moved right; **5.** antler grew.

Hit the Road, *(page 17)* **1.** Biker vanished; **2.** white line filled in; **3.** light grew bigger; **4.** mirror disappeared—watch out for the blind spot!

■ **Best in Show,** *(page 18)* **1.** Part of design disappeared in picture 6.

■ **Pooch on Parade,** *(page 19)* **1.** Dog disappeared; **2.** shorts longer; **3.** leaves disappeared; **4.** heart on hatband filled in; **5.** purple flower grew bigger.

■ **Time to Play,** *(pages 20–21)* **1.** Tail disappeared; **2.** branch fused to trunk; **3.** orange reflector added; **4.** blades of grass grew longer.

■ **Well-Dressed Doggie,** *(page 22)* **1.** Top hat grew taller; **2.** button added; **3.** hole in seat back filled in; **4.** arm erased.

■ **Grin and Bear It!,** *(page 23)* **1.** Flower became solid gold; **2.** bear's paw turned brown; **3.** red collar became black; **4.** some white fur turned black; **5.** gold flower turned red.

■ **Hot Diggety Dog!,** *(page 24)* **1.** Tire deleted in picture 3.

■ **Down at the Dog Beach,** *(page 25)* **1.** Nose turned black; **2.** branches added; **3.** shadow on pail erased; **4.** hole in shovel handle filled in.

■ **Shift into Gear,** *(page 26)* **1.** Black flower erased; **2.** bow disappeared; **3.** bracelet deleted; **4.** silver panel on steering wheel turned black; **5.** rearview mirror moved right.

■ **Let Sleeping Dogs Lie,** *(page 27)* **1.** Tan splotch on sleeping bag disappeared; **2.** more of face became lighter in color; **3.** circle turned red; **4.** white panel of tent turned yellow; **5.** black trim thicker.

■ **Midnight Snack,** *(pages 28–29)* **1.** Bottle disappeared; **2.** fruit vanished; **3.** lemon grew; **4.** orange moved right; **5.** cap became black.

■ **Bench Buddies,** *(page 30)* **1.** Yellow flower turned red; **2.** bolt deleted; **3.** kneesock taller; **4.** bolt became smaller.

■ **Chew on This,** *(page 31)* **1.** Stitching disappeared in picture 4.

■ **Not a Care in the World,** *(page 32)*
1. Tree disappeared; **2.** teeth vanished; **3.** another tree appeared; **4.** red piping removed; **5.** sleeve shortened.

■ **Sea Change,** *(page 36)* **1.** Wave became a whitecap; **2.** bottom of toy boat turned green; **3.** inner circle added to hat; **4.** top of tail turned white; **5.** stone moved right.

■ **Twin Terriers,** *(page 33)* **1.** Foot disappeared; **2.** leash vanished—run free!; **3.** bow missing; **4.** red stripes added; **5.** grass appeared

■ **Behind the Wheel,** *(page 37)* **1.** Mirror arm thinner in picture 2.

■ **Lawn Chair Lounging,** *(page 38)* **1.** Piece added to bar; **2.** armrest erased; **3.** watchband disappeared; **4.** shadow grew darker.

■ **Take a Seat,** *(pages 34–35)* **1.** Brass buttons added; **2.** armrest covered; **3.** green leaf appeared; **4.** rug extended.

On the Dottie, *(page 39)* **1.** Circle turned black; **2.** helmet strap turned yellow; **3.** black spot became larger; **4.** "DOTTIE" moved right; **5.** tail grew.

Bird's-Eye View, *(page 40)* **1.** Pane raised; **2.** parrot grew more feathers; **3.** beak turned solid red; **4.** hole in collar filled in.

Don't Fence Me In!, *(page 41)* **1.** Container moved up; **2.** brown spot appeared; **3.** tail turned solid brown; **4.** spot disappeared; **5.** gap in fence filled in.

Animal Print, *(pages 42–43)* **1.** Dog disappeared; **2.** spot vanished; **3.** spot moved right; **4.** pattern disappeared; **5.** spot appeared.

Orchard Stroll, *(page 44)* **1.** Tree trunk appeared; **2.** tree trunk deleted; **3.** umbrella grew; **4.** more white flowers appeared.

A Plethora of Pillows, *(page 45)* **1.** Dots missing; **2.** stripe gone; **3.** white post became black; **4.** knee moved; **5.** girl's hair grew.

LEVEL 2

■ **Dem Bones,** *(page 46)* **1.** Ear skinnier; **2.** brown patch spread; **3.** the bones are multiplying!; **4.** line extended; **5.** division sign changed to minus sign; **6.** dog became cat—what kind of math is this, exactly?; **7.** another bone appeared.

■ **Morning, Joe!,** *(page 50)* **1.** Flower added to sheet in photo 4.

■ **Pooch Patrol,** *(page 47)* **1.** Shirt lengthened; **2.** more trees appeared; **3.** dalmatian gained a spot; **4.** collar tab shifted right; **5.** boots became *really* high waders; **6.** another bracelet appeared; **7.** tail vanished.

■ **Chill Chaser,** *(page 51)* **1.** Pavement cleaned up a bit; **2.** license plate missing—now, *that* will incur a fine!; **3.** car drove away; **4.** bottom of porch turned black; **5.** sweater gained a leg; **6.** studs added to collar; **7.** headlight added—for increased visibility!

■ **It Takes Two to Play a Tango,** *(pages 48–49)* **1.** Bar disappeared; **2.** radiator expanded— things are really heating up!; **3.** button turned black; **4.** shoe disappeared; **5.** white post grew taller; **6.** triangular piece flipped.

■ **Homework Helper,** *(page 52)* **1.** Pink stripe turned purple; **2.** tail grew; **3.** hair tie turned pink; **4.** pencil became blue; **5.** ponytail grew; **6.** rail disappeared.

■ **Santorini Snoozer,**
(pages 56–57)
1. Board longer; 2. X became a cross—custom grillework!; 3. compartment skinnier; 4. box moved down; 5. stair extended; 6. gray stripe erased; 7. window taller.

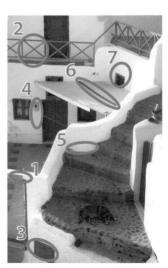

■ **Master Hurdler,** *(page 53)* **1.** Branches disappeared; **2.** red and green cones swapped; **3.** pole lengthened; **4.** ear longer; **5.** front pole moved back; **6.** one red section became white.

■ **Go with the Flow,** *(page 54)* **1.** Fence disappeared; **2.** window taller; **3.** another segment appeared on base; **4.** rectangle became oval; **5.** another spike appeared; **6.** flower gone—water quality issues?

■ **Dog House Delight,** *(page 58)* **1.** Stone area extended; **2.** top of red handle removed; **3.** railing support added; **4.** flowerpot moved back; **5.** black trim extended; **6.** eye uncovered; **7.** part of railing missing.

■ **Hot Dogs,** *(page 55)* **1.** Plant sprouted; **2.** collar turned red; **3.** sandal style changed; **4.** fire spreading; **5.** stripe appeared; **6.** leaf blew away.

■ **Bird-dogging Blast,** *(page 59)* **1.** Pier support longer in photo 5.

■ **Bichon Frise Frame,** *(page 60)* **1.** Leaf grew bigger; **2.** caption missing—apparently, no explanation was needed!; **3.** dog grew a beard; **4.** photo upside down; **5.** pillow became rounded; **6.** flower bloomed.

■ **Crowd Control,** *(page 63)* **1.** Palm tree appeared; **2.** leash vanished—keep an eye on that dog!; **3.** casting a bigger shadow; **4.** shirt now solid red; **5.** shadow vanished; **6.** leg straightened—something stopped him in his tracks!; **7.** picnickers went home.

■ **Glamour Shots,** *(page 61)* **1.** Mat extended; **2.** two panes became one; **3.** another knob appeared; **4.** strap added to sandal; **5.** rectangular inset rounded off; **6.** yellow shirt turned green.

■ **Gate Guard,** *(page 64)* **1.** Rock vanished in photo 2.

■ **Canine Express,** *(page 62)* **1.** Another wire appeared; **2.** tracks removed—the folks who depend on that route will not be pleased!; **3.** more rocks appeared; **4.** vent disappeared; **5.** vents added—for improved air quality!; **6.** more bricks became dark; **7.** post deleted.

■ **Telling *Tails* Out of School,** *(page 65)* **1.** Gap closed up; **2.** hemline lowered; **3.** headband solid pink; **4.** teapot changed direction; **5.** more flowers appeared; **6.** cup and saucer added—are more guests expected?; **7.** fence taller.

ANSWERS

■ How Fetching!,
(pages 66–67)
1. Black bar added; **2.** water level higher—will this result in a bigger splash?; **3.** flag extended; **4.** collar disappeared; **5.** another horizontal bar appeared; **6.** ball vanished.

■ **Playful Par-Tea,** *(page 70)* **1.** Creamer missing in photo 3.

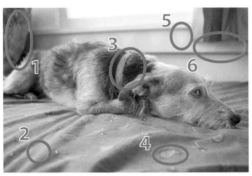

■ **A Tired and True Friend,** *(page 68)* **1.** Blue pillow turned red; **2.** design added; **3.** collar shifted; **4.** design flipped; **5.** white triangle missing; **6.** curtains lengthened.

■ **Watch Dog,** *(page 71)* **1.** Zipper turned brown; **2.** collar turned navy blue; **3.** pants lengthened—to guard against any chill!; **4.** trees fuller; **5.** ear grew longer; **6.** leaf blowing in the wind.

■ **Beachside Barker,** *(page 69)* **1.** Area smoothed out; **2.** person moved left; **3.** dog flipped; **4.** straps disappeared; **5.** wave extended—surf's up!; **6.** backpack grew longer.

■ **Dog Tired,** *(page 72)* **1.** Triangle upside down; **2.** umbrella moved right; **3.** steps added; **4.** chair removed; **5.** boat support added to take load off chair; **6.** post became a V shape.

■ *Chaise*-ing After Changes, *(page 73)*

1. Opening squared off; **2.** paper piling up; **3.** book cover turned red; **4.** latch moved down; **5.** cup turned; **6.** outlet disappeared; **7.** section of building grew.

■ Autumnal Array, *(page 77)* **1.** Leaf turned red

in photo 5.

■ Puppy Love,

(pages 74–75)

1. Snowman missing nose—somewhere, a rabbit is enjoying the carrot!; **2.** branch added; **3.** stars became diamonds; **4.** one plate disappeared; **5.** gold beads removed; **6.** string missing; **7.** fur trim disappeared.

■ Costume Caper, *(page 78)* **1.** Nose squared off;

2. bottleneck grew; **3.** label removed; **4.** hair grew; **5.** glasses removed; **6.** shirt ripped some more; **7.** vents closed up.

■ Grooming Spot, *(page 76)* **1.** Branch removed;

2. stripes turned solid; **3.** flower bloomed; **4.** collar tab longer; **5.** solid trim became dotted; **6.** sock removed.

■ Short Sale, *(page 79)* **1.** Tablecloth lengthened;

2. nails added; **3.** price went up; **4.** bucket moved to edge; **5.** tree disappeared; **6.** green stripe turned orange.

ANSWERS

■ **Saturday in the Park,** *(page 80)* **1.** Tree disappeared; **2.** yellow padding turned red; **3.** tree appeared; **4.** tail grew; **5.** leash handle turned white; **6.** grass appeared.

■ **A Day at the Beach,** *(page 81)* **1.** Pail added; **2.** brown patch grew; **3.** chair grew taller; **4.** umbrella enlarged for more sun protection; **5.** rock appeared; **6.** shadow grew larger—is someone hovering?

■ **Protective Pup,** *(pages 82–83)* **1.** Rail added; **2.** point sharpened for extra protection; **3.** fang added; **4.** "BY" deleted; **5.** ear turned solid black; **6.** post disappeared; **7.** exclamation mark became colon.

■ **Belles of the Balls,** *(page 84)* **1.** More flowers bloomed; **2.** studs added to collar; **3.** cargo pocket disappeared; **4.** paw print flipped; **5.** lavender strap gone; **6.** ball bigger; **7.** cuff turned hot pink.

■ **Throw a Dog a Bone,** *(page 85)* **1.** Chair back became solid; **2.** leg added to table; **3.** post removed; **4.** white stripe gone; **5.** "Kylian" became "Rylian"; **6.** decorative log added; **7.** doorway taller.

■ **End of the Road,** *(page 86)* **1.** Sign moved right; **2.** line grew longer; **3.** hat turned green; **4.** dog now facing owner; **5.** signs switched; **6.** lamp disappeared.

LEVEL 3

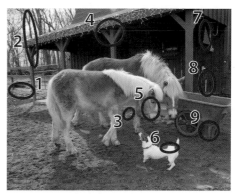

■ **Just Lounging,** *(page 87)* **1.** Bed leg missing; **2.** tree reflection disappeared; **3.** two exclamation points deleted; **4.** mortar line vanished; **5.** seat repaired; **6.** piece now on a slant; **7.** chair leg shortened; **8.** knobs removed; **9.** second strap appeared.

■ **Now Look Here!,** *(page 91)* **1.** Rail added to fence; **2.** tree cut down; **3.** rocks removed; **4.** support squared away; **5.** bridle straps turned pink; **6.** spots connected; **7.** triangle upside down; **8.** handle now on a slant; **9.** wheelbarrow base missing.

■ **Flowery Flight,**
(pages 88–89)
1. Shadow changed shape; **2.** bloom appeared; **3.** garland longer; **4.** leash moved left; **5.** letter A became O; **6.** diagonal bar added to window; **7.** flower picked; **8.** wall plate moved up; **9.** garland lengthened.

■ **High Net Worth,** *(page 92)* **1.** Boards joined; **2.** blue containers turned gray; **3.** wire extended; **4.** flipper lowered; **5.** flag on right of pole—wind shifted; **6.** boat renamed "SPOT"; **7.** round piece squared off; **8.** bolt removed; **9.** windows joined.

■ **Lucky Lookout,** *(page 90)*
1. Silver piece added to rail in photo 5.

■ **Housing Development,** *(page 93)* **1.** Shady area grew; **2.** ball enlarged; **3.** hammer head missing—takes away a bit of its effectiveness!; **4.** red dish turned blue; **5.** letter R became B; **6.** stripe removed; **7.** crossbar added; **8.** handle vanished.

ANSWERS

Step It Up,
(pages 94–95)
1. Roofs joined; **2.** flag blowing in other direction; **3.** plant added; **4.** another stone appeared; **5.** more signs appeared; **6.** dog wandered off; **7.** white wall browned; **8.** wall section straightened out.

TV for Two, *(page 98)* **1.** Vase appeared on TV; **2.** TV turned off—these two are easily entertained!; **3.** leg gone; **4.** wallpaper stripe faded away; **5.** leg grew longer; **6.** lamp shifted position; **7.** black sock turned tan; **8.** clock sideways; **9.** phone removed.

Training Exercise, *(page 96)* **1.** Screens raised; **2.** shorts became pants; **3.** markings switched places; **4.** light added; **5.** sunglasses put on—his future's very bright!; **6.** red flag added; **7.** hat now backward—to match his partner!; **8.** white shirt turned blue.

Playground Pals, *(page 99)* **1.** Crossbar lowered; **2.** part of bar removed; **3.** icon rotated; **4.** tongue back in mouth—he must have quenched his thirst!; **5.** leash pulled taut; **6.** white patch added; **7.** post shorter; **8.** leaves swept away.

Sticking Together, *(page 97)* **1.** Flower plucked in photo 3.

Barnyard Blitz, *(page 100)* **1.** Fence raised—to thwart high-achieving animals!; **2.** overhang gone; **3.** shirt turned white; **4.** support beam added; **5.** girl stepped back; **6.** jeans darkened; **7.** yellow stripe turned red; **8.** board damaged.

The World at His Paws, *(page 101)* **1.** Flag added; **2.** window added; **3.** tail all black; **4.** emblem disappeared; **5.** chimney added; **6.** black spikes turned blue; **7.** another crack appeared; **8.** tree disappeared.

■ **Hydrant and Seek,**

(pages 102–103)
1. Chain longer;
2. grass grew;
3. leaves gone—falling already?;
4. top of cap grew taller; **5.** leash missing; **6.** sleeve lengthened;
7. branch grew;
8. curb covered with grass.

■ **Puzzling Paw-ty,** *(page 104)* **1.** Bottom stone tier gone; **2.** pink circle now orange; **3.** candle added—how many does that make in dog years?; **4.** party hat turned pink; **5.** photo upside down; **6.** polka dot turned into a bone; **7.** pink balloon turned purple; **8.** shadow disappeared.

■ **Pup Tent Puzzler,** *(page 105)* **1.** Black shape added in photo 2.

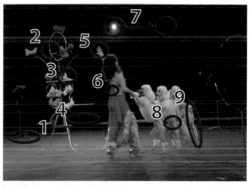

■ **Night at the Circus,** *(page 106)* **1.** Base missing; **2.** birds came home to roost; **3.** bird now facing right; **4.** post added; **5.** hand flipped; **6.** back bared; **7.** light moved right; **8.** fur "coat" lengthened; **9.** dog bowed out.

■ **Welcoming Committee,** *(page 107)* **1.** Third rail added; **2.** houses upended; **3.** part of chair back solid; **4.** doorbell lowered; **5.** wreath moved left; **6.** welcome mat gone—to discourage visitors?; **7.** reflection altered; **8.** knob disappeared; **9.** base missing.

■ **Recreational Vista,** *(page 108)* **1.** Dog now facing right; **2.** controls reversed; **3.** rail extended; **4.** tablecloth askew; **5.** handle upside down; **6.** chair leg added—*much* sturdier now!; **7.** hubcap vanished; **8.** clouds cleared; **9.** vehicle drove away.

■ **Just Horsing Around,** *(page 112)* **1.** More mane in photo 4.

■ **Farmer's Helper,** *(page 109)* **1.** String removed; **2.** brown patch now white; **3.** uppercase letter I became lowercase; **4.** post shortened; **5.** eyes turned green; **6.** button moved down; **7.** polka dots missing; **8.** "HERE" changed to "THERE"; **9.** strand of hair (straw) gone.

■ **Promenade Rambler,** *(page 113)* **1.** Cloud upside down; **2.** facade added; **3.** post removed; **4.** trim painted green; **5.** door vanished; **6.** roof became pointed; **7.** window shrank; **8.** circle became a rectangle; **9.** eave straightened.

■ **Soggy Scene,**
(pages 110–111)
1. Lamppost added; **2.** shawl redraped; **3.** umbrella tip grew; **4.** leaf blew in; **5.** shirt turned green; **6.** collar now red—to coordinate better with leash; **7.** he can't get a handle on his umbrella; **8.** tree added.

■ *Pier*-**bred Pooch,** *(page 114)* **1.** Reflection missing; **2.** shadow longer—was this picture taken later in the day?; **3.** roof became circular; **4.** beam removed; **5.** tree added; **6.** tree bigger; **7.** beams joined; **8.** building appeared; **9.** posts vanished.

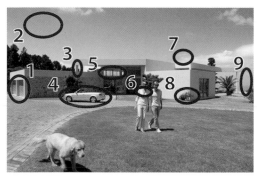

Drive-Thru Service, *(page 115)* **1.** Garage doors joined; **2.** cloud appeared; **3.** post removed; **4.** car turned around; **5.** some panes removed; **6.** neckline altered; **7.** tree appeared; **8.** bush vanished; **9.** pillar added.

Let Them Eat Cake, *(pages 118–119)* **1.** Cake became whole again—how magical!; **2.** tray moved down; **3.** letter C became Q; **4.** fork missing; **5.** fork flipped; **6.** section of lamp widened; **7.** windowpane raised; **8.** tear stain touched up.

Required Reading, *(page 116)* **1.** Bud blossomed; **2.** leaf blew away; **3.** arm curved up; **4.** branch thickened; **5.** pant leg lengthened; **6.** snap added; **7.** spine now matches cover; **8.** part of bench missing.

Street Serenade, *(page 120)* **1.** Handle lengthened; **2.** cuff turned white; **3.** emblem flipped; **4.** hand moved; **5.** string disappeared; **6.** blue tiles appeared; **7.** tiles combined; **8.** part of rope disappeared.

Cruise Control, *(page 117)* **1.** Pole taller; **2.** more paint peeling; **3.** chimney enlarged; **4.** steering wheel disappeared; **5.** dandelions sprung up; **6.** tail missing; **7.** cloud widened; **8.** another window appeared.

Riff Raft, *(page 121)* **1.** Branches pruned; **2.** leaf added; **3.** brown strip turned black; **4.** bandana turned red; **5.** oar gone—they might need that!; **6.** pants turned white; **7.** rock disappeared; **8.** rock added; **9.** more foliage appeared.

■ One Dog Night, *(page 122)* **1.** Outlet moved up; **2.** foot of sofa gone; **3.** stripes added to bowl; **4.** frames switched places; **5.** tread worn off; **6.** paper piles joined; **7.** chair arm extended; **8.** hinge added.

■ Street Stroll, *(page 125)* **1.** Roofline extended; **2.** hat now red; **3.** antenna taller—for better reception!; **4.** brown spot disappeared; **5.** fastener added; **6.** wire strung; **7.** house vanished; **8.** antenna shifted right.

■ Dapper Dogpatch, *(page 123)* **1.** White splotch filled in photo 6.

■ Sheepdog Search,

(pages 126–127)
1. Post narrowed; **2.** cylinder now smoother; **3.** hose removed—hope that wasn't the brake line!; **4.** weave filled in; **5.** light turned yellow; **6.** handle added; **7.** tag added to collar; **8.** cart wall raised.

■ Stair Down, *(page 124)* **1.** Crack filled in; **2.** vent enlarged; **3.** bag missing—stop, thief!; **4.** headphones darkened; **5.** post moved right; **6.** collar removed; **7.** mortar line appeared; **8.** urn taller; **9.** hinges added.

■ Leashed Looker, *(page 128)* **1.** Tree shortened; **2.** tie shifted left; **3.** heel widened—more practical!; **4.** post deleted; **5.** leash handle enlarged; **6.** light upside down; **7.** windows swapped; **8.** door turned black; **9.** lamppost gone.

LEVEL 4

■ **Dogs Agog!,** *(page 129)* **1.** White dog moved left; **2.** tennis ball moved right and down; **3.** dog's tail flipped; **4.** ball turned blue; **5.** this dog's shadow keeps getting bigger and bigger!; **6.** dog vanished; **7.** dog tag larger; **8.** dog deleted; **9.** dogs switched places; **10.** dog moved right and down.

■ **Perplexing Path,** *(page 132)* **1.** Chimney disappeared; **2.** more of wall fell into shadow; **3.** more pink flowers appeared; **4.** another white blossom added; **5.** window moved right; **6.** fence disappeared; **7.** grass overgrew stone; **8.** another plant appeared; **9.** block became bigger; **10.** branches appeared.

■ **Hot Dog!,** *(page 130)* **1.** Paint spatter grew bigger; **2.** white area became pink—this scene *was* lacking in color!; **3.** pink dot shifted; **4.** teeth disappeared; **5.** peace sign became gold medallion; **6.** sleeve lengthened; **7.** speaker screen vanished; **8.** starburst appeared; **9.** blue paint erased; **10.** blue paint spatter appeared.

■ **Hot Chihuahua!,** *(page 133)* **1.** Pavement darkened; **2.** fountain statue removed; **3.** table leg vanished; **4.** fringe added; **5.** fur added to ear; **6.** collar disappeared; **7.** branches added to palm tree; **8.** tail fuller; **9.** cloud disappeared; **10.** cushion adjusted.

■ **Shop 'Til You Drop,** *(pages 134–135)* **1.** Grass patch grew bigger; **2.** branch disappeared; **3.** board appeared; **4.** tree fuller; **5.** diagonal red line on sign switched direction; **6.** hand moved; **7.** pumps turned black—how boring!; **8.** window filled in; **9.** shopping bag shortened; **10.** more purple flowers appeared.

■ **Lying Low,** *(page 131)* **1.** Dress longer in picture 1.

Porch Pooch, *(page 136)* **1.** Railing disappeared; **2.** white area enlarged; **3.** leaves vanished; **4.** hat taller; **5.** white area removed; **6.** branches overgrew porch corner; **7.** plant grew; **8.** some stars vanished—which states seceded?; **9.** tree fuller; **10.** blossom moved up.

It's a Dog's Life, *(page 139)* **1.** Hand brake disappeared—there's danger ahead!; **2.** bar vanished; **3.** seat turned black; **4.** grass appeared; **5.** strands added; **6.** tail grew; **7.** design disappeared; **8.** vents closed; **9.** leaf vanished; **10.** leaves added.

Leader of the Pack, *(page 137)* **1.** Post added; **2.** yellow line disappeared; **3.** lamppost moved left—it's cozying up to the other one!; **4.** palm tree grew; **5.** tail longer; **6.** back of tank top became straight; **7.** light deleted; **8.** cyclist vanished; **9.** overhang disappeared; **10.** black dog bigger—what kind of dog is that?

Rake in the Differences, *(page 140)* **1.** Handle darkened; **2.** band deleted from planter; **3.** flower picked; **4.** blossom turned orange; **5.** glove lengthened; **6.** pink flower appeared; **7.** bangs fuller—she even found time to spruce *herself* up!; **8.** leaves added; **9.** shirt lengthened; **10.** pink flowers appeared.

Polka Dot Pup, *(page 138)* **1.** One dot became bigger in picture 5.

Home Improvements, *(page 141)* **1.** Curtain pulled left; **2.** beam appeared; **3.** throw pillow added; **4.** painting shrunk; **5.** lamp erased; **6.** design deleted; **7.** beam vanished; **8.** dish disappeared; **9.** stand deleted from painting; **10.** knob enlarged.

■ **Dog on Board,**

(pages 142–143)
1. End of pipe turned red;
2. flower became red; **3.** knob deleted;
4. bandanna became solid red;
5. mats joined;
6. step extended;
7. wheel disappeared; **8.** trim turned black;
9. flower image disappeared;
10. handle vanished.

■ **Labrador of the Lake,** *(page 146)* **1.** More branches appeared; **2.** rocks added; **3.** trunk thickened; **4.** tree appeared; **5.** leaves turned orange; **6.** pole disappeared; **7.** trunk jumped right—this forest is enchanted!; **8.** shirt became solid black; **9.** yellow leaves disappeared; **10.** mug enlarged—fill 'er up!

■ **Dog Days of Summer,** *(page 144)* **1.** Cap now red; **2.** peak expanded; **3.** another banana appeared— eat them before they go bad!; **4.** stripe on dog's head disappeared; **5.** cherry tomato turned into a full-size tomato; **6.** cup moved left; **7.** cloud drifted left; **8.** image vanished; **9.** patch darkened; **10.** cup turned blue.

■ **Mush!,** *(page 147)* **1.** Shadow grew; **2.** tree deleted; **3.** ear appeared; **4.** one dog ran away; **5.** leg moved out of sight; **6.** sign moved left; **7.** ear vanished; **8.** tree moved left; **9.** knot appeared; **10.** pole thickened.

■ **Summertime Stroll,** *(page 145)* **1.** Ear deleted in picture 4.

■ **Nobody Gets Past Me!,**

(pages 148–149)
1. More curls appeared; **2.** tassel erased; **3.** table leg moved left; **4.** hat turned solid black;
5. white band vanished; **6.** silver ring disappeared;
7. white splotch turned brown;
8. lips turned red;
9. one display head deleted;
10. diamond shape vanished.

■ Did Somebody Say "Biscuit"?, *(page 150)*
1. Arrow changed direction; **2.** thumb disappeared;
3. brown splotch turned white; **4.** picture vanished;
5. button enlarged; **6.** collar disappeared; **7.** photo
moved right; **8.** bracelets vanished; **9.** image disappeared; **10.** cloud appeared.

■ Horsin' Around, *(page 153)* **1.** Brownish
area turned white; **2.** white area turned gray; **3.** spur
vanished; **4.** dog's head no longer in view; **5.** black
area of fur spread; **6.** another dog appeared; **7.** ear
lengthened; **8.** gray area became white; **9.** horse's tail
grew longer; **10.** brown area of fur spread.

■ Puzzling Plaza, *(page 151)* **1.** Gate extended
right; **2.** roof raised; **3.** tower moved left; **4.** bells
disappeared; **5.** inner square deleted; **6.** bush grew;
7. tree grew; **8.** inner square deleted; **9.** orange base
turned black; **10.** gold square enlarged.

■ Woman's Best Friend?, *(page 154)* **1.** Hat turned
yellow; **2.** windows filled in; **3.** red awning turned blue;
4. yellow fringe disappeared; **5.** button fell off; **6.** ringlet
deleted; **7.** scarf grew longer; **8.** branches deleted;
9. collar turned green; **10.** bench disappeared.

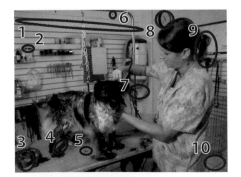

■ Hair of the Dog, *(page 152)* **1.** Wall section
darkened; **2.** lid turned red; **3.** red part of leash turned
purple; **4.** shadow deleted; **5.** tuft of hair vanished; **6.** hook
erased; **7.** vacuum coil appeared; **8.** clock disappeared;
9. ponytail grew bigger; **10.** grout lines vanished.

■ Teatime for Terriers, *(page 155)* **1.** Handle
grew; **2.** flower appeared; **3.** leaf grew; **4.** fabric turned
pink; **5.** center of flower filled in; **6.** nose shrunk;
7. blossom disappeared; **8.** flower turned yellow;
9. checker pattern became solid; **10.** books vanished.

■ **Rise to the Occasion,**
(pages 156–157)
1. Building taller; **2.** ring disappeared; **3.** windows filled in; **4.** top of building disappeared; **5.** container gone; **6.** tail shifted; **7.** container turned red; **8.** black ring appeared; **9.** crane erased; **10.** bottom of boat turned blue.

■ **Out for a Stroll,** *(page 160)* **1.** Wall turned white; **2.** bars appeared; **3.** tail vanished; **4.** horizontal bar disappeared; **5.** leash turned black; **6.** watch moved to other wrist; **7.** black splotches disappeared; **8.** another branch appeared; **9.** small dog disappeared—this walker is falling down on the job!; **10.** tree deleted.

■ **Riverside Walk,** *(page 158)* **1.** Tree disappeared; **2.** more grass appeared; **3.** person vanished; **4.** tail grew; **5.** roof turned white; **6.** window filled in; **7.** jacket grew longer; **8.** more leaves appeared; **9.** leaves disappeared; **10.** window added.

■ **Rein in the Changes,** *(page 161)* **1.** Window filled in; **2.** pole grew taller; **3.** dog grew bigger; **4.** person vanished; **5.** mound of snow grew bigger; **6.** telephone wire appeared; **7.** window moved left; **8.** dog disappeared; **9.** pole vanished; **10.** pole grew taller.

■ **Down on the Farm,** *(page 159)* **1.** More strands added to mane; **2.** cloud moved left; **3.** snow appeared; **4.** board widened; **5.** part of overhang vanished; **6.** sock turned gray; **7.** post disappeared; **8.** ear turned brown; **9.** cloud floated up; **10.** green bar extended.

■ **Down by the Bay,** *(page 162)* **1.** Post deleted; **2.** rock appeared; **3.** sail turned red; **4.** flag disappeared; **5.** gap on cap filled in; **6.** more brown fur appeared; **7.** dog's leg disappeared; **8.** bottom stripes of flag lopped off; **9.** ladder turned black; **10.** pole grew thicker.

■ **Rest Stop,** *(page 163)* **1.** Bar on bench moved left in picture 4.

■ **Not Your Typical Fire Dog,**
(pages 164–165)
1. Steel portion disappeared; **2.** detail added; **3.** handle erased; **4.** bottom stripe deleted; **5.** more stripes added; **6.** writing deleted from helmet; **7.** number 71 on helmet changed to 77; **8.** mustache added; **9.** handle disappeared; **10.** bandage removed—wound healed, just like that!; **11.** grout line appeared.

■ **Westward, Ho!,** *(page 167)* **1.** Bush extended left; **2.** coil vanished; **3.** cuff turned black; **4.** frayed end enlarged; **5.** design deleted; **6.** triangle became tan; **7.** red shape turned black; **8.** tongue pulled in a bit; **9.** leaf appeared; **10.** patch of grass covered.

■ **Don't Be Sheepish,** *(page 168)* **1.** Building extended right; **2.** brown splotch appeared; **3.** post taller; **4.** dog moved left; **5.** panels turned gray; **6.** brown area turned black; **7.** face became tan; **8.** roof disappeared; **9.** branch added; **10.** trunk disappeared.

■ **Take a Walk,** *(page 166)* **1.** Building expanded; **2.** windows filled in—no more beautiful view!; **3.** bush fuller; **4.** leaves appeared; **5.** belt turned brown—less flashy!; **6.** lantern moved right; **7.** branch fused with trunk; **8.** sleeve grew longer; **9.** fence filled in.